Riverside Reflections

Riverside Reflections

Poetic Moods from "The Valley of the Moon"

Harley Brumbaugh

TUSKO PRESS
2533 Ferndale Ave. NE • Renton, WA 98056
(425) 255-9309

Dedicated to
The Children of the Mill...

For information write to Tusko Press, 2533 Ferndale Ave. NE, Renton, WA 98056, (425) 255-9309

Library of Congress Catalog Card No. 97-90715

ISBN 0-9659362-01

ACKNOWLEDGMENTS

An adequate, complete expression of gratitude when compiling a work which has been “in the works” an entire lifetime would be more extensive than the book itself. Better put would be, who is not to thank? For surely all who have shared life with me can be found within these pages in some dimension.. if from childhood, you are their; musician, student, teacher, family, community, school, you are there. I gratefully acknowledge you and thank God for bringing our paths together.

I find certain little people exerting increasing influence upon me. They are called grandchildren with names like Joey, Chloe, Hanna and Austin. I acknowledge our love... and that of their beautiful parents Blaine and Diana; Marc and Heidi.

To my Grandfather, Emery Brumbaugh, whose voice resonated with “”The Face On The Bar Room Floor” and such. To my late father, Aaron “Tusko” Brumbaugh who passed on to me that same poetic heritage...thank you. To my “sister-cousin”, Diane, who as a young girl wrote poetry that inspired me to think poetically....thank you.

Those who have generously given of themselves to see to it that I don't mess up the process of converting words to ink and publication, I stand in awe of your skills, knowledge and art. Jack Evans for being there as a writer, mentor, encourager and guiding light each step of the way! To Michael Jaynes for graphic design and formatting but even more so for your assuring regard for artistic integrity!

To those who valiantly attempted to rescue me from complete breakdown due to embryonic computer skills, you are my heroes - Lee Naasz and Dale Gleason! Dale, for years you were possibly the only person to know I was hooked on poetry. I owe you much...

To Cathy, my wife, whose transforming love has nourished, and sustained, not only our personal and family lives, but that of educator, professional-musician, composer, minister of music, conductor and now a man of literary bent. I am so blessed!

TABLE OF CONTENTS

Village On The Hill

Open Page!

Twin Peaks' Anthology!

INTRODUCTION

What does a musician-educator and yes maybe logger-at-heart, know of the world of poetry? Music and poetry are nearly one! Plato made little distinction between them. The poet- musician by first instinct is a listener... to life... letting the ear do the leading. Leading to a deeper sense teeming with species of silence and song... the sense of music at play with poetry!

And so, I offer words gathered and colored by a rich mosaic of life. A life nurtured by family, friends, and faith, warmly interwoven by the joyous musical process. A life bonded a thousand times over to former students who persist in enfolding hugs in preference to the vacant space of a handshake.

The blessed joy of a childhood lovingly shared, rings at the core of my being! This was made possible by the junction of time and place. The time: mid-century America. The place: The amber moods of meadow, streams and woods of Snoqualmie Valley. Surrounded by mill-town family, molded by impress of war-time purpose, boyhood was a mix of "after-the-war" ideals and Tom Sawyer dreaming. We had no rich/ we had no poor/ We had each other and no locked door... would pretty much describe us.

This poetic window, though somewhat time smudged, and shuttered, illumines what belongs, validating that yes, we are still of a certain place.

This book is not meant for rapid reading. Take it for friendly walks, meandering through open pages... they will love you for it!... revealing more than "surface things"... closely hushed or "widely flung"...,"beneath the cloudless sky" of RIVERSIDE REFLECTIONS...

Harley Brumbaugh

Harley Brumbaugh
1997

Riverside Reflections

Four Riverside Reflections

–To Ed Bassett–
(who cast a cloudless sky upon a boy's destination)

There is in everyone's heart
a calling to the past;
Where youth is but a fragile day
...but then,
No day is made to last.

My day I gave to the riverside
where flows the river by,
Reflecting cedar, boy and fir,
beneath a cloudless sky.

We were there suspended
in silent conversation.
None but the river spoke
of its greater destination.

Time changes things!
it always will...
The cedar and the boy
have long passed...
through the mill.

Beside a Slender Stream

Upon this green bank
beside this slender stream,
slumbers a moment
drifting in a dream...
Music fills the breeze
spreading joy
of humming trees.
Birds are born
to sing of this;
their grandest air
of fluted bliss...

Meadow and wood
soothes the day
It is good...
It is May.

Children Of The Mill

I come to sit in dappled shade
While lingering on the hill.
To gather sounds once made
By children of the mill.

Children of the mill;
You patriots of distant war,
Marbles bulging pockets...
Still you play for more.

'Classroom-cozy'...
Drones the humming mill
Sprinkling cedar aroma
Through speckled windowsill.

Desk-bound dreamers
With singing hearts at play
Facing blanks and spaces...
Filled by close of day.

Here was once a schoolyard
Teeming with youthful bliss!
Here a sling-shot schoolboy
Stole a jump-rope kiss.

Gone the cresting voices
From the school upon the hill.
*Still I am among them;
The children of the mill.

*alternate line: Here, you are among them...
Harley Brumbaugh, 1997

Abandoned Meadow

The meadow on the farside of the pond
has taken to trees!
Not firm, seasoned evergreens,
but spindly vine-maple and early alders.
...When they settled? ...
I don't know
By guess and by growth...
more'n a couple a' crops ago.

No tree alone came to grow,
causing loss of grass and clover.
Thistles too with creeping vine
have somehow taken over!

I can't retrace the pasture or place
beyond last recall of
this flock-filled field
with flowing brook,
still... there is the scent of cedar
riding the warm 'chinook'.

Remember lazy cattle,
gleaning at grazing pace...
where now Canadian thistle
burns the heart
and tears the eye
for want of open space.

Dimpling Day

Day is as youth
holding promise
beyond the hour
with vacillation
of wind, sun and shower.

No man fills a joy
as full as a simple boy
giving splash to a water hole
on a rainy day!
...He doesn't call it work
...He doesn't call it play
Who's to say?

Whether broken or kept,
each puddle is debt.
Too shallow to forgive
...Too deep to forget

Boom-chuck - Boom-chuck
Les Labrie

(The most popular 'old-time' band
in the Snoqualmie Valley.)

Boom-chuck, boom-chuck one-two-three
The one legged drummer
and his orchestry!
He checks the cymbal
and the pedal to his drum;
cow-bell, drum-sticks
the place begins to hum.
Boom-a-chick, boom-a-chick two-three-four
loggers and ladies fill the floor
a boom-chuck steppin' to Les Labrie
The One Legged Drummer and "His Orchestry"!

Boom-chuck slide to "Carolina Moon"
Stomp the other foot with a boom-chuck-boom.!

Farmers and their 'fillies'
drive clean from Tolt
They don't know the step,
but they sure know the holt
as they boom-chuck-a-squeeze
to Les Labrie
The One Legged Drummer and "His Orchestry"!

Boom-chuck-hop its a schottische tune,
Then stomp those boots on a boom-a-chuck-boom

From the North Fork Moose to the Union Hall,
Get your shin-kickin' boots
to the shin-kickin' ball.
Whistle-punk, choker-setters off on a spree
prancin' to the music of Les Labrie...
One Legged Drummer and "His Orchestry"!

Saturday night... is a Si-View dance
Ladies like lovin' and the guys like the chance
To snuggle in a Ford; stash a bottle... pull the plug
pucker-up, and whistle and take another slug
ya gotta "wet your whistle" if you're gonna "cut a rug"!

Then boom-chuck stagger back through the door.
Dance a little 'tighter' and keep a wantin' more
of boom chuckin' music of Les Labrie
Boom-chuck, boom-a-chick... Yes-sir-ree!
The One Legged Drummer and "His Orchestry"!

Exotic Boxcars of 1944

(Riverside boys taking "the tracks" home from school)

Feel... the ground tremble and rumble!
...with ears to the rail we hear approaching thunder
of steel upon steel- iron upon iron!

The crescendo mounts, the wooden ties
groan under screeching sway.
Another huge, black locomotive, dressed
"fit -to- kill" in its finest cow catcher
clinkin'-clanks to the mill.

Far away places... unfamilier unfurl;
emblazoned upon parading brick-red boxcars:
Baltimore... Milwaukee... Atlanta...
Wichita... Boise;
They skate upon our silver tracks
What little we know of destinations
We all shout back...
"Maryland!... Wisconsin!... Georgia!...
Kansas! ... Idaho!
Yours are places we shall go !
But..., what if we can't get back...?

Once we placed a penny on the railroad track
...didn't make a dent in your "clickety-clack"
or "clunkety-rattle",
tot'in timber to Tacoma and Seattle...

Why do most trains go
a 'tootin' a caboose to Kokomo...?
Tempting boys along the way
to hop-on freight-car dreams
of "get-away"?

'Bet Miss Bennet Knows
where evr'y train track goes!
She's our teacher from Georgia.
an' talks sorta smooth and slow...
bet she knows how to go to Kokomo...

Hidden Meadow

Showing overgrowth of neglect,
A rutted trace of tractors and wagons.
Dips through the grove to connect
the field to an otherwise hidden meadow...

Entering... it is hushed
with quiet beyond silence.
Framed by flaming maple
and cottonwoods.

Late September
cradles the mountain
in Autumn shroud

Such soft stillness...
no hush no whisper
the river, summer - slender,
lullaby hums.

May I pass through?
...changing little as I do
oh, maybe color a cloud or two
no more, no less
leaving the hue of nothingness...

Hide-and-Seek

Where is the child, who once was?
Who dared to reach for rainbows?
Where is he... that seeker of truth;
who saw beyond
a callow youth
Where are the bright stars...
Where are the rainbows...
Where is the child?

Where did it go? That "deep-within"
coloring Riverside dreams?
Is it in turn, the lad who speaks
of the man outgrowing joy?
Who is "it" plays hide-and-seek
Eluding the man by hiding a boy

High Expectation!

The nine-summer, valley boy
balanced the rails
most of a mile!

LADIES AND GENTLEMEN,
BOYS AND GIRLS
YOUR ATTENTION PLEASE!
HIGH ABOVE CENTER RING,
FEARLESSLY BALANCING ON
ONE SINGLE STRAND OF SILVER BEAM,
THIN AS AN ARROW,
COMPLETELY BLINDFOLDED,
WHILE PUSHING HIS PRIZED DOG
IN A STAR-SPANGLED WHEELBARROW!

then... something between
stumbling and stepping down
lost his fanfare fantasy
to a waiting circus clown...
...too much was high
...too much was straight
...too much was narrow
*for a dog to hitch a ride
in a wheelbarrow.

*alternate line:" for a boy to give a ride"

A Fleeting Stay

A tempest breeze...
the mood turns chill.
a swirl climbs higher
...'till
On sweep of sudden gust
an eager flake
comes riding in!
whirling and twirling
feathering a dance
flirting by nature
but settling by chance
in the lap of the river
leaving it...
spotless

Man of Milk and Music!

In loving memory of
-George Swenson-
Ode to his joyous delivery!
Mid-century, Snoqualmie Valley

On prime valley days,
if mood be still...
Lingers a wisp of music
from far upon the hill.

A faint warble... whistling,
gathers a tinkle -of - bottle -tune
Sprinkling "Zip-A-Dee-Do-Dahs"
with a bit of 'Crosby-croon'.

His joyous praise belongs
to ripened fields and Riverside.
Counting blessings, rolling along
his milk and honey ride!

Bounding stride and cheerful eye
gladdens the road each passes by
As milk bottles dance quick-step style
To the Monte Vista Man
with the Van Johnson smile.

His singing heart and boyish grin
Bids," Friends and neighbors, join right in"!
..."Lift your voice and sing with me,
Our greater joy is yet to be!"

Sharing dreams is a thing of bliss.
Let us build, beginning with this.
Listen for the voice upon the hill.
...The man of milk and music...
from the farm above the mill.

Harley A. Brumbaugh
September 8, 1996

Melon Ripe

(Highland Drive - Harvest Moon)

"Thar's gold in them thar hills."
Is the promise of the day!
Against the sheen of evergreen
It could be no other way

There is gold in hidden hills
While Autumn hosts the night.
Yellow drips and juices down...
Our Moon is melon ripe!

A Meadowbrook Morning

Late June 1944

Early morning... the team of huge Belgian horses
exit the massive red barn set by the river.
Delaying first at the watering trough,
clop and harness-jangle their way across
the paved intersection
allured by promise of open fields.

Rudy, the blacksmith, solitary resident
of the derelict old Meadowbrook Farm Hotel,
stirs the day with ringing "clunks"
of mallet upon anvil.

Soon, trafficking mill workers rumble the bridge,
on way to another "knot-hole- grabbing" day.
The loggers, headin' for "the woods",
by now, are crew-truck rattling
mountain- bound toward "Old Camp B".

The Trailways bus
(older locals still call it "the stage")
passes through, wending its way up the hill
and down again to the mill,
captained by "Driver- Bud".
Aboard is the morning Seattle "P.I."
bearing banners
of the latest from the war - front!
The several local "paper-boys",
bicycle-ready, greet his banter and cargo.

Ol' Doc Templeton is making
early morning rounds at the
Hospital crested on 'Nob-Hill'.
Tholo, his assisting nurse,
readies his Meadowbrook office
for the day's succession of
aches, pains, complaints
check-ups and emergencies.

Meadowbrook Main Street:

The Men's Store with the
old Scotts Taylor..., Watch Repair Shop.
The Tavern..., Harry's Barbershop
Koontz's Mortuary and Ambulance Service
...the Corner Service Station
Brown's Meat Market... Grocery Store
Doc Tennant's Dental Office...
Ladies Dress shop...
Tavern...Almond's Drugstore
and Brook Theater

Crossing the street to the south:

The brick building housing
The General Store,
Furniture and Appliances
and equally bricked Meadow Brook Hotel...
Housing several of our single school teachers.

Country-cozy, this
village of Meadowbrook, home to
a few more than a hundred valley folks,
mainstreet- measures one-hundred and twelve
full boyhood strides.

Though coming days would reduce her
to high-ballin' "Harleys" an' tractors
...This day, dressed in pastels
of Meadowbrook mellow... held her.

The Joy of "Kick-The-Can"!

-Dark lesson of a Riverside game -

Shaded memory falls open.
The faintest self,
...near vacant,
leaves the flesh behind...
The joy of "kick the can"
What is this to me...
this complex that I am?
Mending soul and spirit
at the thought of "kick-the-can"!

The joy of "kick-the-can"!
Stalking in shadows, timing his strike.
What of this could shape the man?
The games he would play
throughout the night...
jaded memory falls open.

Grace

Who dares so much

as to touch

This delicate dandelion?

It far exceeds

Most other weeds

By simply never tryin'...

Fishers Of Men

(Incident on the middle-fork
of the Snoqualmie River)

He fished the streams...
climbed the mountain
By light of summer sky.
Drank from rivers
of crystal fountains
And chased the butterfly.

Butterflies feast the eye
by field, stream and brook...
But don't apply
as worm nor fly
Upon a baited hook!

He left the rod upon the sod
to cup a butterfly.
...While kneeling there,
somewhat in prayer,
Released it to the sky.

I often yearn to return
to this summer fishing day.
Where once again
the boy within
Shows the man the way.

Matinee

At the "Brook Theater"

Matinee lovers seem to know!
'Chancing' to meet at a Saturday show,
brings "puppy-love" hearts to tremolo.
"Puppy-love" lovers grow weak-in-the-knees
simply holding hands with a now-and-then
squeeze.
By popcorn agreement and studied pose
whispers and silence open and close.
Something of this lingers today...
What more could one ask of a matinee?

The Maple Leaf Twirl

October's 'gust' near the Meadowbrook bridge

Much, too much dance...
Much, too much swirl...
Flouncing and flitting
The Maple Leaf Twirl!

See... a floating leaf
Settles to stay.
But one quick gust
Scares it away

Storming wood-winds
Blow brash..., blow stiff
"Howlin' and a hootin"
A "hootenanny" riff!

Shuffle and shutter,
Strut and drag...
Syncopatin' branches
Beat a "Maple Leaf Rag"!

Keepsake?

...JANUARY 1950...
Meeting on a school snow-day
What else is there to know
But mitten-in-glove through the snow?
Winter white is cold and deep.
Nothing here will we keep

...JULY 1951...
Below the Falls
Hush... here on the river beach
Ripples giggle each to each.
We hum and sing "Don't Cry Joe"
We held this day... but then let go

...SEPTEMBER 1952...
Below the Falls
A rising rainbow paints the sky,
Beyond our grasp... is left to dry.
A halo-rings the mist and spray
But just as soon... went away

...DECEMBER 1953...
Ellensburg
The blush of clover reaped the rose
As seasons and hearts opened and closed
The years turn over and forever sleep
...something of this was meant to keep

Legacy

(The Valley of the Moon)

What can I do...
Lush Valley of the Moon?
What to return?
...You nurtured my greening days:

Clinging vines do grow
once held to memory
of midnight moons
above a Mount Si snow.

What must I do
to preserve sacred a place?

...oh, so gently

and swiftly

slip away.

...yes...

slip away.

vanish

without

a

trace

Baton Twirler

(Remembering a lovely girl - Sharon)

Outside... the woman
Inside... the girl
Peddle-pushers and baton
Learning how to twirl

The last love to vanish
Was the first love of her youth
Whirling round and round
and hand-to-hand
The staff of balanced truth

Live and learn,
Twirl and toss
The higher the throw...
The greater her loss!

What remains
of majorette loveliness?
A single year-book autograph...
"...Could you really love me?
...please don't make me guess."

Lamentation of the Shaman

(An ancient Snoqualmie)

The Sun sends forth the essential
Coaxing all before it... Rise!
The Eastern Mountain thrusts forth
its response...
Precipitous rock inner bursting, thrusting out
Thrusting out the river utopian
Catching its sudden fall
Trusting valley breeze
to stir wind-ward the wolfen call.

From cosmic companion to spheres Universal
Celestials to earthen understood.
The pillared voice, millennium repeating
"It is good... It is good!"

Ancient of the Snoqualmie,
Long-sleeper 'of the moon',
Loosen your guttural chant
of anguished quarter-tone.
Rise smoke-ward across vanquished years
Keen deeply for stricken streams,
Bleeding from mangled mountains... make long lament!
Shaman of Antiquity, your fading voice grows still
Smothered deeply in bitter of cold cement...
Though I stand where once you stood
I have no voice to say "It is good..., It is good"...

Lady Water Lily

(The Indian Slough)

By darkened lake
where no light fills the valley floor
she spreads her breast
to the sycamore
succulent moist,
lily-brimming,
unfolding charms
of languid swimming.
Fold upon fold
of golden shaft
pierced the dark
when e'er she laughed
at rippled desire.

Her watery world,
of shimmering womb
bears its fruit
then floods the tomb.
Though it be love
that makes me cry,
I shan't reveal
the water lily's lie.

My Meadow

(By right of deepest need)

This meadow is mine!
Alive and innocent.
Here, I gave my youth...
Now, all that was is spent.

Hear the meadow lark's
...Antiphon of truth!
So pure; her blessed sacrament...
of meadow, brook and youth.

As valley meadows shrink
from over-growth of greed,
Remember my plea to stake a claim
by right of deepest need.

Mimic the meadow lark's song?
Is merely mocking truth.
...Mocking the fading memory.
of my meadow, the brook and a youth.

The 'Riverside Rats'!

Hey Fred, My dad said we can have the old chicken coop!
So, with shovel and hoe, while holding our breath,
(The recent flood had claimed all but the chicken-poop)
The boys of Riverside took quick deed to "The Shed"

By tacit agreement it was acknowledged
Those desirous of membership
Must prove worthiness by sacrifice
of scrubbing, painting, building bunks
and yes, scrapping off still more
dried chicken shed souvenirs!

All qualified boys immediately proclaimed
Noble and prideful right of exclusive membership
to the "Riverside Rats"...
Open to the entire known world
With the proviso of rightful residency
of Snoqualmie Falls, Washington
with specific lodging and allegiance to
neighborhood of "Riverside" and its
closest environs be sworn to and verified!

With the ceremonial posting of two signs
deemed essential and sacrosanct reading
"THE RAT SHED" and "NO GIRLS ALLOWED"
The boys entered into the proclaimed
world headquarters of "The Riverside Rats"!

Each lad built his customized bunk.
For day-time lounging or overnight stay.
Posting guard of overnight vigils
To keep members in, and phantom girls at bay.

Duly elected, charter officers included:
Bruno - President; Fred - Vice-President
Harley - Treasurer
(No one wanted to be secretary...)
it seemed too sissy! So we had none...
All other vital roles were filled by:
Eugene, Lyle, Johnny, Gene and Dave
These were the Riverside boys
Of the bicycle brigade!

To create and sustain the treasury,
primary means of fiscal support
was dependent upon regular deployment
of bicycle brigades roadside foraging
for "dead-soldier" bottles.
To be sold and resold to Meadowbrook taverns.
First, as-is dirty!
Second, sparkling clean
and unrecognizably scrubbed.

Peeling cascara bark,
Digging dandelion roots,
Logging cottonwoods
kept coffers filled
by stacking wood
and stockpiling goods.

These days of variegated puberty
were spent in neighborly mixes of activity:
Fall - football on Riverside Corridor
last days of fishing.
Winter - sledding, skateless hockey on Indian Slough
rainy walks up to the "hall"
Dancing, skating and basketball!
Spring - Trout fishing, marbles and baseball.
Summer - crew-cuts, River swims, bean picking,
sword-fern fights and all-weather bicycling
All subject to stop and start by
a mother's call of mill-whistle consent.

Some now and then events...
football games pitting
Riverside against "The Orchard"
Sling-shot shooting across the river
countering Meadowbrook boys
invading our trestle.

We were early mud-ball slingers
in tree-trunk stumps
Defending Riverside in fox-hole trenches
and hand molding clumps
of clay

Builders of rafts on Meadowbrook Slough
Binding logs to floating planks
Or anything "grounded" upon its banks
These were our: "Tom Sawyer" ways
But days of thinning ranks.

By rush of hormonal decision
The boys began to agree
The cardinal of "NO GIRLS ALLOWED"
Be interpreted a bit more leniently!

By allegiance, each river boy
became a Mount Si "Wildcat"
But by truth of heart
he remains a part
of the one and only pack,
a SnoqualmieFalls, "Riverside Rat"!

Plank-n'-Board

(To my imaginative young ears, the aggregate music of the mill was the ostinato drone and cadence of "clink-chanks" suggesting the repeated dirge "plank n ' board"... etc.)

The slicing ax and saw
Raped to inner-core
The bloom of virgin woodland
'till it could bleed no more...
"plank n' board - plank n' board"
cross-cut cadence grieves the Lord!

Nash of teeth like slash of sword
Pillaging the forest for...
plank n' board - plank n' board"
cross-cut cadence grieves the Lord!

Cathedrals steepled by
Ancient Nobles brought down for...
"plank n' board - plank n' board"
cross-cut cadence grieves the Lord

Over-growth chokes
A ghostly stump remains
Marker of past paradise,
grave-stone of the slain...
"plank n' board - plank n' board"
*cross-cut cadence grieves the Lord
cross-cut cadence - plank n' board
grieves the Lord - plank n' board
**a... cross...

*slowing and hushed
**hushed

Playmate

(The Riverside cottonwood grove)
shortcut to the "tracks"...

Still stands the mingling grove
With path for idle day.
Through shedding cottonwoods
One can trace the child's play

He has no need of playmate
Here, no need of toy.
The hidden voice of ample spring
occupies the boy

The few who seem to know him
somehow find it odd.
He claims to never play alone;
but always plays with God!

River Wading

In the
Middle-Fork River
opposite the Norman-Brook Farm

I delight myself in shallow
drifts of river sand.
No lasting print be made...
No lasting mark of man

As I'm witness to the vanishing
My care is all for not.
Nothing sets- a-drift
Like current river-thought

I shall freely celebrate
the sacrament of water and sand;
And step-by-step, thrash about
The bliss at my command!

Scout Troop Four-Ninety-Two

(Dedicated to the memory of the six killed -
while serving in World War Two...
William Borden, William Hronek Jr., Bernard Briggs,
Frank Martindale Jr., Jack Dubey and Lloyd Scheel)

To the mill-town that squared them right,
To woods that made them brave,
Scores of "tender-foot" soldiers now spend the night
With the six they could not save

From Europe to the Pacific
This valley's blood was shed
Fighting for Snoqualmie Falls, America!
Now... warrior and town are dead

We pledge by pieces of mill and town
For those they served in war
To never let their mem'ry down
Nor this, the land they perished for

As "God Bless America" rings!
O'er vista of mountain view
Forget not, those voices who no longer sing
...Six Boy Scouts of troop four-ninety-two...

Night Shade

"Snoqualm"
1712 a.d.

Life is perceived

As the moon...

Full, Ripe...

Framed by Silhouette

of Firs

Still...

The ripened moon

casts the deepest

shadow...

Inner-Space Voices

(To those belonging to Snoqualmie Falls)

Longings from the inner-space
usher from boundless deep;
Voices once familiar
rousing from their sleep.

Outer-bound to silence...
Inner-bound to fear;
Dumb be the darkness
we alone can hear.

Faint and distant echoes
unveil the mill-town cast
Still... nothing here removes
The yearning for the past...

Oh, to hush the longing
seeping from the soul
Of ever-folksy voices
gone so long ago.

So... we linger here...
With hands and hearts embraced
Sharing pain of still belonging
To a vanished town and place.
Swept away by sweeping change
We know of bitter-sweet wine
and hemlock's after-taste:
The agony of belonging
to a town of people
speaking from
hush of inner-
space.

Mount Si Pageantry

My soul leaps when I behold
lofty reaches of Mount Si...
so it stood, as I began
so it shall, when I die,
leaving whatever sacred be
among her cliffs
of mystic pageantry!

There... variegated moods
are more than passers by;
giving mounting flare
of jagged edge to
slope of Eastern sky.

O'er sheer walls and cliffs
and tumbling boulder
She drapes off-and-on rainbows
haloing her head and shoulder.
Of steeping verity
I cling to her purple moods
of mystic pageantry!

Rain-Bell

(Spring rain pelting an old rusted cow-bell in a long-vacant field, 1966)

Rain rings the rusted bell
Lying as an empty shell.
Each stroke of sound
Spills o'er the ground
...Rain-bell... ring!

Seasonal cadence of the rains
Taunt what last remains.
Rise up! Ring, ring for Mother Time
Your last cow-bell chime!

Rain takes its toll at last
As if to wash away the past.
Rain-bell ring!
Rain-bell... ring...

Pick A Promise

I have the need to run again
through fields of boundless sky:
To pick a promise from the brook
and pile the promise high!

I have the need to fly again
through fields of blissful chance:
To skip a stone across the blue
and sing the ripple's dance.

This, a taste of heaven
and what it is to die:
I fling myself across the brook...
...God plucks me out to dry!

Mill Town Dreamers

Mill Town Makers...
You dreamers of dreams
Nurtured in fields and forests
By pools of lakes and streams.

Players, moving measure by measure
squeezing the juice of 'Mill Town' pleasure
Some, there were of great renown
from "The toast of Hollywood!"
To the toast of a ghost of a town.

In another time,
when those of yesterday
and tomorrow meet...
(On some providential corner
on a particular pearly street)
Will there be inherited purpose
or another judgment day...
counting our chips or turning away?

No turning!... We are dove-tail dreamers
...a tongue an' groove timber-town,
Strong builders of solid beams!
Bolster-laminate when need be...

Allowing no splinter or knot weakened seams.
One generation standing raw-boned tall
upon squared shoulders of another
building links as sister and brother
Framing foundations of family upon
love of Father for Mother!

Mill Town Makers...
Dreamers of dreams
of fields and forests,
of rivers and streams...

No Return

What night has written
Day cannot erase.
Still, deep waters gather
In another place.

What tumbling shallows take
They never do replace:
That's the pity of water.
That's the pity of haste.

Riverside Garden

-In memory of Anna Anderson-
...celebrating her garden hospitality...

Come to my garden in afternoon days.
Come to my garden of blossoming praise.
Rest 'neath the willow's soft, dappled shade...
Blessings, we'll gather, in cool of the glade.

Here, velvet petals smile at the sky
Soaking in sun's four o'clock high!
Apron gath'ring we shall go
Daffodil yellow in blue calico

Enter the gate left open for you.
The berries are plump and blossoms new
Vines ripe with all they bear
Give fragrance to a Riverside prayer
Apron gathering we shall go...
Daffodil yellow in blue calico

Opus!

Inspired by the teachings of
Charles Scott,
(First Choral Director of Mt. Si High School)

Song is Life!... Life is Song!
Upon a single Breath a world is hung.
A note taken in...must then be flung
From innermost to outermost!.

The measure of man,
if their be need,
is weighted by treasure,
or gift of deed.

Men of melody rise and fall.
Yet, rising again, trumpet the call
To the victor's throne!
Where whimpers no sound of monotone.

Celebrate the lasting joy!...
Music making man in the heart of a boy!
Sorrow of sorrows is a seedless thing:
a shriveling world without the joy to sing...

Porches And Sheds

to neighborly porches and slated sheds
of Snoqualmie Falls, Washington... gone

All that is good, all that is fair
Somehow seems to linger there.
If such a joy be set apart...
A home there is within your heart!

Vacant boards cannot contain
What's meant of love to sustain.
Porches and sheds will not agree...
But a home in the heart will always be!

A Valley Woman Sings - 1873

To inspiring courage
of pioneer women of the
Snoqualmie Valley

A valley woman sings
Her open lonesoming
As long-stemmed shadows
Choose an Eastward way
She tends her garden
To close the day.

A lonely woman hums
Yet, feels the need to cry
To far horizons
Her amber lullaby

The valley woman sings
Her simple nurturing
Lilac calm fills the air.
Her soothing voice...
A garden prayer

Refraction Of Season

A season beyond climax has a truth...
If truth prefers moderation,
It is clouded by extreme sensation.

Truth In Season
Winter - when putting storms to rest
Spring - still blooming, but bursting less
Summer - by degree, wears her cooler dress
Autumn - seeking leaner lines, reveals herself

It is not the taking in...
But, the giving up!
"Forsaking all others..."

Straddlin' Zephyrs

-The souls of horse racers of the Snoqualmie Tribe, upper prairie-

You've gone,
gone a ridin'
racin' through the heavens.
Leapin' clouds
astride cayuse zephyrs
a stirrin' up stardust
...Ride On!...
Bare-backed an' showin' yer heels
to a million planets across the spread
...Ride On!...
Painted ponys, ears back, manes a flowin'
and Snoqualmie Proud!
...Ride On!...
You displaced sons
of a thousand ancient snows
Now you go hell-bent for leather
chasing your Valley of the Moon
...Ride On!... Ride On!...

Surface Things

A scene from the Reinig Road

Early Autumn without rain
sets pools apart.
The river bank shows a gain
since summer's lazy start

Too much sun makes a river sag;
loosing ripples to a shallow snag.
But, surface babblings do conceal
What deeper, longer looks reveal.

Honest things need not hide...
Where is truth, if not inside?
River life at thirsty autumn
Shows the heart from top to bottom

Times there are, we stand to gain;
...to find oneself in need of rain

Wind-Fall

The lone, windfall hemlock, uprooted,
braced itself in limbs and arms of branches
closely held by a long-standing maple.
Here, the "widow-maker" came to rest...
cradle-held from sixty-some seasons
of neighborliness.

Each strains against "dead-weight"
...holding the other.

Soon, December's wind and snow
will strike her final blow

Then both hemlock and maple will go
...embracing

Life passes through arms of another:
one common grave... one common cradle
...one common mother.

Pot-Bellied Stove

Nothing draws a logger like a pot bellied stove...
It is center universe...
Throwing a glow upon his greater
treasure of things.

One such center piece
is in the "filers shack"
Mid saws, files, ax-handles and blades
Stands the pot-bellied stove
Keeping the remnants of
the morning's coffee
Growing more bitter by the moment,
but still providing excuse for bull sessions
set ablaze with tell-tale stories
taller than Paul Bunyon's 'peavey'!

Tales of hook-tenders, fallers, riggin'-slingers,
'bushlers, choker-setters, buckers and
the latest "green-horn"
The bull-buck of the pot bellied stove
stokes the fire that stokes the tongues
of these spinners-of-yarn.
Snoose-chewing Swedes and Norwegians
getting a temporary hand up on the other.
Spit-tune laughing at Einer, Ole, Casey and Shorty.

The pot bellied stove brings
its own music to the woods.!
knitting reels and yarns
to "git-fiddle" goods...
Foot-jigging tales of days gone bye.
Coming to rest on a bunk-house-lullaby.

Visionary

The edge of sky
is the inverse horizon!
Hazardous, the day overcast...
lacking reference other than self.
Shrouded contours do preserve
promises of warning wishes
glimpsed against haze
of filtered truth

Trail of Compromise

An attempt to retrace a long-lost river trail

Within the overgrowth lies a field of sunken
orchard.
I find no ready-made way welcomes me.
Not far in, a faint hint of trail beckons.
Only to vanish in a den of salal and undergrowth.

In short time all trace of destination become
swallowed by aimless swamp and springs.
No trails lead... all trails must follow
either by trick of light or shape of things.

Retracing, I discover two parallel paths.
One, well worn, the other; not yet broken in.
Straddling the old and new.
where valley traits shape the rivers' bend.
I near my journey's end

Planting feet where two paths meet
Speaks more of truth than compromise
Where the river greets *Swenson Creek.
I found the way by bright and sunny skies.

*Now known as Brockway Creek

Winter-moss

I shall recall this, a life- time hence...
Caressing green mosses
Clinging to upper reaches of this windfall.
Which yesterday brushed winter sky...
But deeper evening brought freezing gusts
enough to lay her low.

Cool moss of the north side..
First and last I am,
To stroke your fibrous crown
Seventy years above my reach
Within a moment, sudden...
Split-shushes down.

Cracking woods now silent
In crush of heavy snow.
Place the blame to life itself
Soon, I too, shall go...

Three Score And Ten

-Less than a life-time was the longevity of Snoqualmie Falls, Washington-

Three score and ten
is but a fragment of time and space...
Yet greater than the remains of this place.
Named for the river that falls to the sea
This is 'home'... and will always be.

Established upon vast cathedrals
of ancient evergreens,
Our timber-town stretched from now to eternity
(or so we're raised to believe)
Within a never-the-less life-time, however,
Was stricken to become a nursery...
Vacant of "timber-barren" apology.

Forgive us for not inviting you in
But callused 'progress' has done it again;
Cycles of the restless growing apart
Losing a home that hides in the heart

Tapestry

These woods are ripe with song
hung upon silent tapestry
all things here belong
so... where can the Weaver be?

Lacing threads of time
through space and energy
He spindle feeds with giving breath
the heavenly symmetry

He weaves upon the master loom
the spider web and Milky Way:
Fathomless depths from riverlets
and man from a lump of clay

Who sees in all design a single tapestry
finds as much as can be made
of God's locality...

Village On The Hill

Village On The Hill

(Snoqualmie Falls, Washington - vanished)

Alone with the river in shade cast
by the derelict trestle,
I lose most of the afternoon to meandering memory.
Gathering my own remains of
vanished places, fading voices and dimming faces
The jealous temperament of Nature
where men have taken up...
She in turn erases.
...much as tracing the silent notes of a lost flute.

<u>Beside the trestle</u>

This very spot of some fifty summers ago
was fit for skipping rocks across the current.
The flatter the better for bounding the river flow.

<u>From sycamore junction 'turn-around'</u>

A sudden voice startled the quiet!
"Which way to the Falls?"
Called a young man lending support
to a dismounted bicycle.
He wore a slight smirk
knowing full well he had intruded
upon my slumbered reflections.

"Take the road veering to the right of the bridge -
It'll keep the river to your left.
And the Mill Pond to your right.",
I replied by reflex
of long years and boyhood habit...
"You'll come out on the old "Sunset Highway"
From where the roads meet you'll see the lodge
a quarter mile up to your right."

"So where does this upper road lead?"
"Takes you up to the mill", I answered,
"What mill"?, he replied.
Choosing talk over yelling
I stood to narrow our distance.
"Say, if you've got a moment or two
I've a need to talk with you...

Ya know, not much to see but a little
water leaping over the Falls this time of year.
I'd best show you around my "what mill" town.
I need to talk of what's left of home
...of what I'd call my own.

From the lightening scarred fir tree

Leave your bike in what once-upon-a-time
was my front yard,
Rest it against that lightning-struck fir...
Deeper in overgrowth,
hides a chestnut , maple and mother's holly

Facing North

There now; devote a moment
with eyes closed and ears open...
Picture here, snug cottages on tree lined lanes...
From this open corner
the road takes leave of
river warble for the drone of the mill.
Maple, elm and Sycamore in off-and-on seasons
dress and undress
This is "Riverside"
couldn't call it more, or by name nothing less.

Facing Mt. Si

Why whisper-talk? I don't know...
Deepest instinct tells me though.
Mysterious hosts of Heaven bless
deeper sleep as loggers rest.
'Neath shadowed peaks of Mount Si
framing horizon of Eastern sky

Filtered through over-growth
August neighbors cool in front-porch breeze.
...Screen doors and window plants,
opening memories.

Open your eyes gently
To the village on the hill.
Here, a man's a logger
or worker in the mill.
Open your heart to see
What can be made of it still.

Enter 'Sycamore Corridor'

From where we stand in the open
"Riverside" reaches to
Swenson's Creek
Beside each home a sycamore.
Sheltering a bike or swing
The shaded road... a football field
When Autumn has her fling.

Return to Sycamore Junction "turn-around"

In the hollow cradled
by the bend in the road here
Stands the building clustering
neighborly garages.
The school bus and Trailway "stage"
stops here to fatten loads
That cherry tree overhanging the garage
is ripe both for the eating and the climbing
Playing hide-and-seek or kick-the-can
Closes a day of summer tan.
What makes a house a home?
People... people with a liking for one another!
Each with a roll vital to the other.
Families: Martin, Lawrence, Rice,
Briggs, Folsum. Brumbaugh, Nelson,
Anderson, Sterud, Margreiter, Emmerton
Webster, Eades, Monnot, Olsen, Roth
Francis, Wagner, Simons, Peoples,
Rice, Reeves... many more

buying their "goods" from the company store...
Solomon, Francis, Poe, Pierini,
Darst, Eades, Shepherd, Wagner,
Kelly, Boyle, Matchesnik, McQuade,
Jernberg, McGinnis, Platt,
many more....
Workin' for the end of a World War!

Behind each home
Stands a slatted shed
housing stacks of fire- wood
be it green or planer-end
Pat Cambley drives the "wood-truck".
Dumping two cords
stretching mid- Fall to early Spring.
Stacking and choppin'...
A mill-town boy is understood
To keep his back-porch brimming
With kindling and fire-wood...

Progress up the hill

Notice, young friend,
We have little use for fences.
Can't think of anyone
we mean to keep out...
Free to come and go
Free to move about!
Seems to me barriers
are cause for round-a-bout.

Beyond the slight left turn in the road

Strolling further up the hill: Hear it?
...it's the droning of the mill.
To our left, over the bank
where Ivy snuggles the trees
Are "Railroad Avenue" neighbors.
The tracks run between them
and the Mill Pond.
If you've a mind for danger,
can tread the backs of logs
from shore to shore.
McGinnis, Bliss, Platt, Rutledge
Funk, Leeder, Rook,
Since the war, log and freight trains
don't mind 'wakin' people anytime of night.
It's not those that pass through,
but those that choose to rumble back and forth
switchin tracks and takin on more cars
headed for God-knows-where
that shakes the windows and doors.
All the houses share the hill as a back yard.
Some keep a few geese and ducks
between them and the tracks.

Proceed to mill access road

We'll take this road to the left...
down to the mill.
Look off here to the right
To the red fire shack and the green garage.
They serve "The Dirty Dozen".
Was there ever a mill that didn't send out
smoke stacks of soot?
Here, flocks of cinders make smooth landings,
gliding in graceful, swirling motion...
But wayward winds with different spins
give gritty flits a whirling-dervish notion!
The Mayrands, Wools, Hills, McDonalds
Felix, O'Neils and McFarlands
are neighborly here...
"Close to work, close to school."
Even the women folks often
take the worn-path which skirts
the company Barbershop
clinging to the hillside half-way below.

At mill office, turn to face immediate steep bank

The ancient barber is George Stephen
born nearly a century before.
He tells of first crossing the river by canoe!
He, market bag in hand,
cheerfully walks his way to work
from the hill beyond Riverside
and Indian homes.

In the meantime...
on downward stairs,
we stand face-to-face
to the company mill.

Facing the mill

The large, cedar-shake building
standing to the left, houses "Head Offices"...
managers, superintendents ,time-keepers
that kind o' lot...
Men on the green-chain call 'em "pencil-pushers"...
"pencil -pushers" who went off to school
So as not to have to work for a livin'.
You can spot e'm...
Spot their lily-smooth hands and dressed-up,
downtown look!

Progress North about 80 yards
(The store faces South)

Across the large parking lot to your right
dressed in matching shakes,
is our Company Store.
Spread across the front is the massive
porch, gouged unmercifully by calks
of loggers' boots. That smaller door to the
left is the Post Office serving the Mill and town
of Snoqualmie Falls, Washington.
Mail arrives daily on the afternoon bus
from Seattle. Each household has a "box"

safely kept with secret combination locks.
Box 121
Snoqualmie Falls Washington.
psst... two after c-two after-t
Each finger-tip klick... unlocks a mystery.

Just inside the post office door are
posters describing...
"Man wanted" for offenses and crimes
mostly unknown to these parts.
Outside, in that window-like case,
are the weekly posted photographs
taken by Harold Keller, Manager
of our Community Hall.
He records in black and white display
Our mid-century community...
not so much for now, as another day.

As we enter the company store
You'll see ev'ry thing that meets
a working man's fancy.
Oh sure, some goods and groceries
are scarce... rationed because of the war effort.
The gover'ment issues rationing stamps
making sure no one "hoards" from another.
Nothin' very fancy; just basic
clothes, shoes and boots,
hardware, saws, axes, sporting goods,
some furniture.

Most put it on-the- tab
till draw-day.
The store office,
at the head of the stairs up in the balcony,
is where Bill Hronek
manages things.
He's got Wagner, Kelly, Torgeson
minding matters.
Plus several of our high schoolers learn to work
filling phone orders and
driving the old delivery truck.
Unless someone's in a real pinch,
You'll find it right here...
oh, once in a great while ya might
jump in the car and drive clean
to North Bend, that is if you couldn't
find it first in Meadowbrook or Snoqualmie.

With your back to the mill and facing the hill
through the grove of trees
trace the shorter hillside-steps to
the Boarding House

This is where "the singles" live.
or those of vagabond bent.
One of the company rules
"No liquor, no booze".
Sometimes when short-handed
Art Benson drives to town
To make do with skid-row help
Picking it up wherever it landed.

The boarding house becomes home
to such folks, but usually not for long.
Most boarders are hard working
Many nights pass in cards, guitar and song.

What keeps these men here a workin?
Food... plain and simple...
and lots of it!
The "chow-hall" doesn't put up
with deep conversation
...mostly "pass the... what-ever" underscored
by tinkling spoons, forks and knives.
Simple talk from simple lives.

That long stairwell climbin' up that steep hillside
takes ya up to the social center of our community.
We just call it "The Hall"
We'll take the long way up and around
the road.
The houses here in "the Gap" are generally mid-management.
Nice big lawns with shade trees. Families like the
Emmertons, Westerlund, Herferth,
Spjut, McBain and such.
Winter-time and this road becomes the best darn
down hill sleddin' around these parts.
Starts at the very top up by the school and it's free going
clean down to the parking lot down to the mill.
The tilted grade around this hair-pin curve adds to
to the speed.
Best years for sleddin' I can recall was back
in 'forty-six and winter 'forty-nine and fifty.

Progress to Ivy covered retaining wall
on left - face overlooking the mill

We're comin' up on the second home to most kids here.
It's the Community Hall.
The big covered porch there shelters a lot
of roller-skaters on Saturdays... waitin'
to be let in. Harold Keller manages
"The Hall"... strict, fair, and friendly and I might add... safe.
Let's go inside ' show ya around.
To the left inside the main door is the office.
Ya check out the roller skates here.

Across the lobby is the pool room,
Ping-Pong table, checker boards
The double door opens to the gymnasium.
Kids play basketball by the hour. Of course they have
volleyball, skating and gymnastics here at different times.
The Halloween and Christmas parties are a delight
The balcony is for observing games and
in the far corner is the record player for music to
roller-skate to.
Ward Keller draws duty from
his Dad to change the stacks of
old 78's organ records.
If we step back into the lobby again,
I'll show you the auditorium.
First time I saw television, other than
for the Indian Head test pattern was right here
watchin' Clyde Lovelett play basketball
for one of them Kansas schools

Saturdays Harold Keller shows serial movies here for
the kids, usually have an industrial film and an old
black and white cartoon. They have to stop
ev'ry now and then to change reels. That's when
selected neighborhood kids get to perform some music
for the rest of the community. Good little,
musicians and singers.
This auditorium is used by the school across the
street for singing classes and some movies.
The union sometimes has meetings here.
First magician I ever saw was right on that stage.
Eunice Keller dressed as a Halloween witch
shreeked an' cackled so that I 'bout wet!
Got so scared the tears rolled right on down my leg.!
If we head on down the stairs we'll see the kitchen to
the right.
The larger room is for banquets and socials
dancing class and after-game highschool 'mixers'.

Let's stroll down the hall here a bit.
We'll pass assorted meeting rooms.
here to the right is a branch of the
Methodist Church Sunday School room.
The Ladies Music Study Group and here, Boy Scout Troop
four- ninety-two meets weekly... Lot'a boys spent their
"tender-foot" days a tie'n knots. Six of the boys, two of
'em Eagle Scouts, never made it back home from the war.
What a shame... some of the valley's best!

If we exit this side door at the end of the hallway
it'll take us to the head of the steps clinging
to the hill leading back down to the mill again.
No need to take those ninety-four steps down.
Means another ninety-four comin' back up again.
This room on our left as we step up the side-
walk is our community library. School kids
moms and dads and boarding house men
browse for reading and resource
materials here. Its been said our kids here read a lot.
Some more in summer than during school months.
Well, lets head up across the parking lot
Up to the School...

Enter the schoolyard beyond ivy retaining wall facing east.
The yellow wooden school building is directly to your right

The school yard at the back of the school here
has a sand box by the bus-stop...
tennis court in the middle there is usually
used for "kick-goal" The monkey-bars on the far
kitty-corner at the foot of the steep
bank is guaranteed to place blisters
and calluses on youngsters.
The row of houses overlooking the playfield
is "The Terrace".
The upper play ground extends around the other side
of the building... mostly baseball played there.
Hit a ball over the hill was almost always
good for a home-run unless it was retrieved
by a real slinger like Neal Moses!

This sidewalk along the back side
has seen and heard a lot of hop-scotch squares
and jump-rope-ditties.
The first door is to the Boy's Basement...
used for poor weather recesses.
The farther door is the Girl's Basement...
...skirts and blouses, but mostly dresses.

Progress south, toward curve in road

The middle door here serves as the main entrance to the school.
It leads up to the second floor where the classrooms are
located. Dasn't take two steps in one bound
or you'll have to face Miss Seblen
The rooms are located pretty much as to grades.
These first rooms are the lower grades...
progressing to higher the further down the main hallway.

To the left

The lunchroom, which also houses the school
library features the friendly smiles and fine cooking of several of
the community ladies.
Peanut butter and honey sandwiches are daily fare.
Potato salad beyond compare!
The principal's office to the left... up a few steps...
the music room... Mr. Bassett comes each Tuesday
and Thursday to teach beginning "horn-honkers" here.
We also show our educational movies in this room.
If we have special events we take the kids across the
lot to the community hall and use their auditorium.

The gradeschool basketball team uses the hall's gymnasium.
Works out real well.
Directly across the hall is a special room . Miss Moss holds
classes for kids needing special attention in reading
and spelling... We'll go through the front door and
cross the street to spend a few minutes
wandering over "Nob Hill".

Locate cement steps to the hospital lawn

Some choose to
call this "Snob" Hill... cause this is where the
folks paid to make big decisions are
expected to live.
The big structure is the Snoqualmie Falls Hospital.
Built by the persistence of Mr. Warren.
Lots'a baby's drew their first breath here...
On the other hand, some mill-hands and loggers
have also drawn their last...

Some of the life-saving operations performed right here
create quite a medical stir... When all others give up...
you can count on Docs. Burke, Templeton, Max, and Cheney
to come through with a last-ditch miracle operation.
Taking these concrete stairs to the upper lawn. you can
see the "Warren" Monument. From here you see the
Men's Ward on the third floor to the far right and the Women's on
the same floor but to the left. Private rooms are in the middle.
The elevator is located in the middle there.
If not for this hospital, I
would have been a goner... back
in 'forty-five think it was

Face south-east

Notice the large, classic homes neighboring the hospital? As I said earlier, these houses are for those who over-look the rest of the community... just as the houses over-look the mill and woods. The very largest two story house with the columns belongs to "Tip" O'Neil... He's the Superintendent of the entire shebang! Others who qualify to occupy the hill include, Phil Hogan "Boss of the woods" Harold Keller, Manager of our Community Hall.

Up the hill, beyond the crown of the hill, is Monte Vista Farm. The Swensons own and operate it. Mostly dairy products. They truck deliver all over the valley... homes, markets, stores and eateries. Say, if you get the chance you should get-a-load of Mount Si from there!

Returning to road - continue north

Let's push ahead to "The Terrace". Don't seem to have as many kids as most. 'Bout the only area where the little women ain't lookin' across to her neighbor, 'cept down on Railroad Avenue. Sure handy for the school kids here. Most go home for lunch. Ya know, Miss Ella Raines, our very own Hollywood movie star was raised early-on in one of these Terrace homes!

<u>Progress to fork in road take left to intersecting road</u>

This road will take us to the last direct neighborhood
of the mill-town of Snoqualmie Falls. It's known
as "The Orchard"... Lots of kids

...largest cluster of houses of any...
Seems most move to other areas of our town
when available... don't know for sure though
Notice the huge company log trucks runnin' through the
neighborhood, kickin' up a lot of summer dust.
The Gere family lives here to the right. Got lots a company with the
Jordans, Meldrums, Loves, Kelleys, Kantolas, Wrights, well
I could go on but...
Lookin' back to the south of us
you can see that "Orchard" folks get a good
back view of the mill below.
Just beyond, off to the west of the mill pond
you can make out where "Jap-town" used to be.
They lost their homes 'bout eighteen years before
the rest of us.
"String-town" was strung right along the
railroad tracks at the base of the hill.
They were 'bout the first to go... mid-twenties
I reckon... outside plumbing, ya know what I mean.

Just beyond the orchard, 'bout a quarter mile or so
up that road headin' toward the north-west
is the company dump.
Target shooting and rat shooting passes the week-ends
Nothin' much bigger than a "twenty-two" though.

If ya were to stay on that road long enough you'd circle
right on back to "the falls" just where ya tried to head for
in the first place!
We'll young man, I... wanted t' tell... er... what the...
...where'd he run off to?
He just ups and disappears on me!
When he pulled that shenanagin, I don't know.
More 'n likely while I was a trying' to point to
something that needed a pointin' to.

Well, I guess he means to show
he knows what he wants to know
Just a word a caution though...
Nothing stays without land or timber!
I meant to tell him so...

The day came to close
with his eyes lifted to the mountain
of a million melted snows.

Open Page!

Open Page

Upon a wordless page
The meandering pen makes its way.
Tracking residue thoughts
of yesterday.

A poem is born
When made of these...
fragments of fragile memories

As Eagles Dream

As amorous birds of prey
We shall seek our fill this day;
Feasting upon nipplets
of swollen parts
Pulsing as one
of opened hearts

This day of frenzy love
seizure of soul
not spoken of...
passion sobs
for ripened clefts,
with flaming tongues
of openness

Lies the open fruit
juicing of fount and stream,
breathes the scent
of languid kisses
waking from twilight dream

As the lofty eagle
spreads to open wing
We shall probe horizons
Tasting joy in ev'rything!

LIFE...

THAT SACRED SPARK OF EXISTENCE
BEYOND ALL UNDERSTANDING
RIGHTFULLY BELONGS TO
ALL CREATURES...

Nothing, there is,
as profound and deep
as baby's breath
upon the cheek...
...nor
such misty-warm
when springs a sudden leak!

Lady of Dakota Dust

(mother - 1909-1965)

Her "Ma" had no sweetness
But did have a "cocked-eye"
from strings of strokes.

No one had a notion
When Ma's fits of anger
would burst open.
What little she spoke was fuss.
giving way to buggy-whippin'
her kids of Dakota dust.

Ma commences a-whistlin'
or hummin' her dreaded
prelude to a beatin' for no reason
but for dust-bowl-fever-wearin' thin
in the heat of the season...

Alice; tall, sun-freckled with full auburn hair
the older of two younger,
cookin' for full threshing crew;
while she went starving
of a different hunger.

A nine-year-old prairie girl
cooking for hungry prairie men.
from pre-dawn to evening dark
then... over and over and over again.

Made wise by nurture of pain.
This dusty Dakota flower
Came to bloom in Snoqualmie rain
Too soon plucked mid a summer hour...

Fulcrum Point

What keeps such a place?
A humanity void... nothing space.
The less-than-final balance
Puts Man beyond the fulcrum point
Of his own...
There, nothing is returnable.
There, nothing is learnable.

What is gone, is gone...
Leaving the wanting-most
To uni-suckle the global breast.
Her ravished nipples
Shrivel beyond return
To vanish beyond request.

Jewel of Jeopardy

Lone flower, clutching
to rim of formless sea...
You Bloom!
Long-stemmed "Jewel
of Jeopardy".

No purple-stained bouquet
colors the world for me
As does your sweet, disordered
nobility.

January, 1997

Clock

Metered measure of life
Leaving tick-tock traces
Slicing moments by numbers
with silence it displaces.

The world...
A tick-tacky-time-bomb!
If not for love
and Timely graces.

NOTHING NEUTRAL!

LUMINOUS COALS FROM THIRSTY SOULS
BURN FOR THE LIVING WORD.
HEAVEN LIGHTS THE EARTHEN NIGHT
THE MORE THE HEART IS STIRRED.

YET... A TIMOROUS TONGUE
PROCEEDS A TEPID WAY...
LEAVING EDEN EMPTY
WHERE GOD AND MAN WOULD PLAY.

WHO SLUGGISH SINGS OF HEAVEN
STRIKES A DEVILISH NELL
ROUSING WAITING LEGIONS
FROM DEEPER REGIONS OF HELL.

SO PRAISE, YE NOW, THE GOD OF MIGHT
FOR THE RANSOM OF HIS 'WORD'
HEARTS OF MEN AND CHRIST UNITE
WHERE BOTH ARE PASSION-STIRRED!

I AM NO NEUTRAL SINGER!
THE CHOICE IS HEAVEN OR HELL
THE LORD INHABITS HIS PRAISES...
THERE IS A WORLD TO TELL!

Lyla

(Infant sister... taken)

Too soon you sleep, sweet Lyla
Too soon, your deep return.
"Dust-to-dust." heaps mocking cliché
upon hearts of grieving burn.
Unripened child-hood play
chokes the soul as no other way.

Soon I sleep, little Lyla
Soon I slip away...
then again, sweet Lyla,
then, again... we play!

Kiss The Good Night

What of this day I do not see
...I shall never see.
What of this day I do not touch
I shall never touch.
What of this day I do not feel
...I feel too much

Kiss the good night
To welcome tomorrow:
A daily farewell
...More in joy than in sorrow

A Tarnished Rule

Who follows a downward trail
Of shadowy ill intent
Finds the gully full
Of thorny consequent.
An empty cup for a twilight thirst
Does not explain
Why every path is not a first,
Nor ev'ry stride a gain.

Those who plant their feet
Where two ways meet
succeed in compromise.
The root concern
Is full return
To partial paradise.
Another way: Is to say
(tarnishing the golden rule)
"Never take what is to give;
or don't what is to do."

Soaring!

Inspired by and dedicated to
Dr. Wayne S. Hertz

I'm drawn to those who warble...
Who praise with open throat;
Whose music fills the upward sphere
On wings of song and hope!

I'm drawn to those who soar...
On loft of open sail
With flutters and flings
Of out-stretched wings
Face the howling gale.

I'm drawn to downy nesters
Who keep December warm.
With leaves and rigging
Of mosses and twigging
Snuggle in chilling storm.

A Soul set to singing
Flows an upward way
Soaring beyond the setting sun
He leaves no final day!

Thistle and Thorn

Thistle, thorn and cocklebur
  such as these, I am.
Pulling shoots of greening grass
  for the great I Am'.

I wince in pain of devil's club:
  bleed from piercing thorn.
Scathing thighs upon nettles
  where thistle scars are worn.

Never by intention,
  yet... somehow by design,
I lose the way to higher ground
  where thistles do not climb.

What to avoid alters
  what is left to seek...
Elusive roads to heaven
  await the blessed meek.

Adam fell...
  from a God-forbidden tree...
Leaving thistle, thorn and nettle
  and plenty of company!

Monterey Bay

(Lover's Point - Pacific Grove , CA.)

Vast blue, ill-defined,
pulsing ever-birth.

Surface empty, belly-full
each ripple... a universe.

Morning-mix of vapor
erases horizons more

Moving ancient mountains
closer to your shore.

Avoiding lines and edges
by seamless froth and foaming

You sift the sands of Monterey
while searching for Wyoming!

Chasteless Child

What God has written
Man cannot erase!
Trusting hearts are smitten
By burn of false embrace.

I know the deep dark waters
of murky, acid guilt
I drank them in as babbling streams
of deceptive songs of silk.
I am the chasteless child
who grieves the chasteless man...
crawling the endless spiral
where chastity began.

This, the point of healing,
This, the light of light
...I must return where nothing is
before I spend the night...

Candles And Mistletoe

(Lyrics)

Candles and Mistletoe
Soft, falling winter snow...
It's time for love and Christmas

Cranberries, pumpkin pie,
Mem'ries of years gone bye...
It's time for love and Christmas

Loved ones gather 'round the tree
Singing carols in closer harmony.

Moonlight by fire-glow,
Long walks through falling snow...
It's time for love and Christmas

Cookies and candy-canes,
Frost tracing window panes...
It's time for love and Christmas.

The Hedonist

I come to gather grapes.
no reason, but for mirth:
to pluck from pregnant gardens
where willows sweep the earth.

I dance among white lilies.
and sing My need of song...
drink the wine of mortals
defy the glimpsing dawn.

of this I am companion...
of this I celebrate!
to live for tears or laughter
or die from fear of fate.

vacate now, the vineyard
while I intoxicate My breath
I have no need of healing
and see no need of death.

Fragments

My heart is made too much of you!
It is not the thinking thing to do.
Shattered crystal stays that way...
Mixing dreams with broken clay
A fragile thing when kept "for good"
Is held the less... once understood
Bits-and-pieces will have to do.
My heart is made too much of you.

Have Yourself A Day

(In Happy Memory of Dr. Merle Landerholm,
First President of Bellevue Community College)

Have yourself a day without a cloud
Have yourself a day without a crowd
Sing yourself a song you've never heard,
Unless you got it from a humming bird.

Like a meadow lark has joy to sing...
Let yourself go and spread your wings
Across the sky the sun rolls by.
Have yourself a day!

Sunshine, blue sky... love's ev'rywhere
Sea breeze, green trees... you can share
A silent prayer while you're there
With ev'ry blade of grass and silver brook,
It's a natural Mass , without the book!
Dancin' in the sun, you'll discover God's a lover...
Have yourself a day!

Lyrics
1976

The Cleansing Day

With trees bent down,
this becomes my weeping day.
Heart-floods of past "what-ifs"
rise about... seeping through endless,
inner walls.

No gentle cleansing this:
Ripping fibers of remorse, uprooted...
pulled-out... set free
flung far to the outermost!
This day of mix-and-match
carries my soul; to dreamless spaces...
of anguish behind wash-and-wear faces.

Hold the flame to the demon choir!
Heap no more upon the blistering fire.
Take the licks and don't complain
Become more than a trinket
On some Evolutionary chain!

Waltzes and Roses Ago

Lyrics
For Herman and Miriam Schodde
-Fiftieth Wedding Anniversary-

Blossoms of roses fade with the past
Melody lingers, but never to last
In ev'ry rose I behold you.
With ev'ry waltz I still hold you

A rose must remain for its season...
Only to pass with the snow
Still, I will love you, as I loved you,
Waltzes and Roses ago.

Day after day, moment by moment
Bouquets, we gathered for two.
Each, a dream of a moment,
Waltzes, Roses and you.

Trumpet Man

To the memory of Don Anderson
magnificent man of the trumpet!
(Mentor and teacher)

He opens the worn case
slightly aware each latch demands
his open touch.
But, having received... responds.

Within, a road-weary trumpet
snuggles among assorted mutes.
The horn, is cool to his touch
as if being roused another "gig" too much.
By habit he strokes each valve
To sense their mood.
Do they dance, or do they brood?

Placing the trumpet to his lips
(something between giving and receiving a kiss)
He breathes a breath of life
and enters the mystic bliss:
The issue of life is begotten of tone!
...more of his Maker than of his own!
A 'trumpet man' is nightly reborn:
dancing his soul
through an open horn!

...Inspired by Debussy

Her limpid flute
sails upon vapored wings,
...free floating,
among beginningless strings.

Melody and Memory
is a fragile blend...
The lesser part is music,
The greater part... 'friend'.

Twin Peaks'
~~Apology~~
~~Pathology~~
Anthology!

Twin Peaks' Anthology!

Poetic response to Hollywood's dark
setting of the Snoqualmie Valley !
by
"The Twin Peaks Poet"

No one sees, no one speaks
Darkness lies below "Twin Peaks"!

The closer the crime
The better the clue.
This town is "Twin Peaks"!
Who the hell are you?

"Dam'n good coffee!"
"Dam'n good pie!"
Dam'n good place
To live an' die...
Laura was nervous
About meeting "J"
Too soon was the night
Too late came the day...
The darkened music lights the clues.
A Road House dancer feels the "blues".
It's ladies choice... but he must choose...

Josie Packard and Harry S. Truman!
Oh well, our trusted sheriff is only human.

The beast of beasts, you'll never catch
Until Nadine removes the patch
It's less than fashion, yet more than a scratch.

Extract the "R" beneath the nail.
No job too small for all detail
Return again to the railroad car
Look again for the letter "R".

Has Dr. Jacoby been with Laura?
He lost a patient, but not her aura...
In caverns deep below the Falls
The spotted owl and raven calls...
Ancient rituals of sacrifice
Sends a soul to Paradise.

A deposit box at seventeen?
Ten thousand dollars and a "flesh" magazine
...Laura Palmer, Home Coming Queen!

A lonely road beyond the mill
After the picnic (before the kill)
The hooting owl haunts her still.
Lower the casket into the grave...
Now Leland... that's no way to behave.

A piece of pie and an ice-cream sundae
Sharing the paper with Theodore Bundy

Empty hearts with passions filled
Fills the void once blood is spilled
Land of logs and a few stump ranches...
Lonely loggers take their chances
Road House music across the track
A Road House girl on her back

The "Log-Lady" will have no lady log!
Her mind and soul is mist and fog...
She cradles her love but in return
kindles an ember with love to burn...

It started as an innocent prank.
(a little party on the river bank)
Skipping rocks and skipping school
Throwin' stones at the "golden rule!"

Nadine, are you certain
cotton-balls make a silent curtain?
Norma and Ed... you're no longer simply flirtin"!

A "Twin Peaks" Party?
Young blades spittin' sparks
Ax-men makin' cutting remarks...
Paintin' the town and raisin' hell!
Twenty minute dates in a cheap hotel.

All those hours turned into days
setting Kathryn's passion and mill ablaze!
Up to the peaks in search of the dream...
Down to the river to silence her scream
The lady and log together will be
Fueling passion from one family tree!

Dear Special Agent Dale Cooper:
How "Twin Peaks" is blessed...
You deflect bullets with a bullet-proof vest!
You gave us a start but now it would be best
If your next assignment was "Falconcrest"!

Sweaters with "Twin Peaks" are nothing new...
Why, Marilyn Monroe had 'em in nineteen fifty-two!

BIOGRAPHY

Born in Renton, Washington, Harley moved to the Snoqualmie Valley, ("Valley of the Moon") as a youngster. He is one of the "children of the mill" reared in the mill town of Snoqualmie Falls. There, he led a mid-century, "Tom Sawyer" existence as one of the "Riverside Rats", a friendly group of coming-of-age "Riverside" boys.

Driven by love of music, he began playing trumpet professionally by age fourteen. His athletic interests were simultaneously encouraged, primarily due to his 6'4"" frame.. He worked his way through college by "choker-setting" in the "woods" during the summers and year-round professional trumpet playing.

Upon graduating from what is now Central Washington State University, he played full time as a "big-band-on-the-road-musician. After being rescued from 'the road' by the army draft he became an educator, combining professional playing and public school music teaching in such places as Ketchikan, Alaska; Port Angeles, Washington, Renton and Bellevue Community College. Notably, his college vocal group "Celebration" earned international acclamation through world travel and international television.

He has sung and played professionally with the likes of The Seattle Opera Association, The Seattle Symphony, and scores of "name" show-biz personalities.

Honors bestowed upon Harley include: International Who's Who In Music; "National Outstanding Educator" and "Lifetime Achievement Awards."

Throughout his boyhood and career, "the Valley of the Moon" has been his haven. A place to reconnect, to "gather a seed" of a poem, plant it, nurture the thought, allow it to grow and bloom then simply "pick the promise"!

His poetry has appeared in regional publications, as well as "World of Poetry Anthology and "Treasured Poems of America". Riverside Reflections is his first published volume of poetry!